THE RED LIST

THE RED LIST

A POEM

STEPHEN CUSHMAN

LOUISIANA STATE UNIVERSITY PRESS

BATON ROUGE

Published by Louisiana State University Press
Copyright © 2014 by Stephen Cushman
All rights reserved
Manufactured in the United States of America
LSU Press Paperback Original
FIRST PRINTING

DESIGNER: Mandy McDonald Scallan
TYPEFACE: Whitman

Library of Congress Cataloging-in-Publication Data

Cushman, Stephen, 1956–
  The red list : a poem / Stephen Cushman.
    pages cm
  ISBN 978-0-8071-5689-6 (pbk. : alk. paper) — ISBN
978-0-8071-5690-2 (pdf) — ISBN 978-0-8071-5691-9
(epub) — ISBN 978-0-8071-5692-6 (mobi)
  I. Title.
  PS3553.U745R44 2014
  811'.54—dc23

                    2014000834

THE RED LIST

PART 1

Endangerment's foreplay en route to extinction
often but not always. Ask the bald eagle,
ridiculous nickname for that elegant hood
rhymed with its tail, a matched set distinctive
against distant spruce, white as the transit
of pre-dawn Jupiter's super-heated drop
soldering sky plates to cement a meridian;
ask the white hoods about last-minute comebacks,
all but erased by really fine pesticide
but now off the red list and suddenly nemesis
to the gull population, herring or black-backed,
whose chicks make good snacks during long days of fishing.
Eagles increase, local gulls dwindle, till one day, who knows,
seeing an eagle skim low overhead, no bigger deal
than seeing a crow, so what, who cares, the national bird,
as in permit me to flip you the.
                              Move forward as the way opens.
But will the way open? Will the endangerments
prove passing fronts, slow-moving, stalled-seeming
for months, even years, but in the end ushering in
survival's high pressure? Or is this the one
there's no coming back from? And what kind of danger?
The one of tonight they'll drag me away,
my remains in a pile of anonymous others,
or that of believing I have no connection
with someone who's, what, fill in the blank,
male to my female, old to my young, light to my dark?
Connection, praise connection, I'm always connected,
says Hannah, 13, and there's more life on line
than for those who are off, who don't have a life
or really exist. Tell it, little sister, whatever one thinks
of eagles and Jupiter and a parallel universe

where nothing plugs in, the urge to exist
engines most urges from the gull and the eagle
all the way up to you who discriminate
between mere existence and really existing,
no exception made even for the urge,
when existence gets sickening, to endanger oneself.

Ooh, lighten up and give us a break
from these blocks of long lines, we don't have all day
and no one's entitled to jumbo attention
even from throwbacks who still can sustain it
instead of yakking on the phone while navigating traffic
or texting on the crapper or, Hannah, does this happen,
poring over some small screen while taking it from behind?
You're too young to know, one assumes, and, boy,
your parents hope so, but that would be a question
arising from your assertion: Do the connected do it now
like sailors in rough weather, one hand for you,
one for your ship, that glowing device? Could be nice
in some ways, the distraction, perhaps, slowing things down
so no one lapses prematurely and two can synchronize,
thanks to messages back and forth,
RUT   ILBL8   UT2L   SRY   B2W   THNX

Dirty Martini

For this lip-reader
olive juice is hard to tell
from an *I love you.*

One's distraction's another's aphrodisiac,
so who can say that connection here can't enhance
connection there or that texting jimmy
while banging johnny won't turn all on
and move the earth
                          as the earth moved Tuesday,
day before yesterday, 5.9 on Richter's scale,

Charles Francis, born in Ohio, Hello,
I'm a seismologist, what about you,
are you a seismologist too, as if getting paid
to track our temblors weren't cool enough,
you also get to say I'm a seismologist,
never felt the earth move? here lemme help,
don't speak English? no problema, sismo,
Erdbeben, maanjäristys, tremblement de terre,
whatever you call it it jostles us all
thirty miles from epicenter, teenage kid
with three life sentences, middle-age lady
with daily radiation on top of her chemo,
premature baby urgently delivered
to intensive attention, and connects us all
for thirty seconds, even someone standing
alone in the woods while the woods roar and rumble
the sign sufficient, the message received.

The national bird,
Washington's white monument,
has closed for a crack.

Wonder what the eagle's doing
to ready for the hurricane, prophesied for Sunday
and bearing a name that might make one ask
if people paid to christen storms, yet another job to envy,
have anhydrous senses of humor or nasty knacks for irony
or plain don't know Irene means peace; it's sure peaceful now,
blue morning in the buff, not the fig leaf of a cloud,
not a single stitch of wind, for the forty she's left dead,
the bozo on the Outer Banks who thought it boss to surf,
the guy who fried while wading to save a small girl stranded
by waters hiding wires, the many hapless felled by trees
crashing in windows, dropping on rooftops, swatting cars
like blood-puffed mosquitoes. What are you supposed to do?
Act like a bozo, something may happen; act like a hero,
something may happen. But sitting quiet in your room,

minding your own beeswax, when suddenly, pow, you're history
gives Pascal the lie. Death, Leading Causes of:
accidents rank third for men, for women sixth, but rule out
anything having to do with booze or with some kind of machine,
narrow it to nature, in her high assassin mode, e.g., falling tree,
falling coconut, lightning strike, landslide, avalanche,
tornado, flash flood, earthquake, tidal wave, meteor debris,
and the number must be pretty small, especially for those,
neither bozos nor heroes, who keep to little rooms
meekly hoping to miss misfortune. And yet it happens;
shut-in, agoraphobe, convict under house-arrest,
the deeply depressed who sleep all day with sad heads covered
share endangerment, too. Wonder what the eagle's doing.

The white fog covers
island contours like the sheets
drawn over faces.

Move forward as the way opens. And if it can't open
beside the sea or in the woods, perhaps it opens,
in project or penthouse, trailer park or tract development,
with a story instead. Today another aftershock, 3.4;
yesterday the queen of Sheba came to test Solomon
with spices by the camel-load, gold and flashy stones,
but he answered her questions, showed her his stuff,
lots more opulent than hers, knocked the wind right out of her
before he sent her home again with all she could desire.
Odd transaction. What's her game? Show him up? Put him down?
Is this how monarchs pass the time? A shrewd investor,
maybe she figured on a good return in a bearish market:
Bring King Solomon X in gifts, your retinue groaning,
and you go home with ten times X. Or maybe she was angling
to make herself his newest wife, number seven hundred and one,
not exactly top of the heap but possibly a notch or two above
any one of his three hundred concubines. Or maybe she really
needed his help with questions she couldn't answer, like Why,
if you're smitten with foreign women, haven't you come to me?
Am I so ugly? Look at this; take a peek at those. Here we go

into apostasy, hand in hand, just say the word and we can build
a very high place for my abomination. If so, did he say no,
and she chose to attribute a failed seduction to something
she called wisdom? Solomon's sharp, no doubt about it,
that prayer for discernment ranks near the top,
as does his judgment between the two harlots, and don't forget
he built the temple. But all the excess, whether in women
or conspicuous consumption, while slobbering after other gods
when one was taking such good care of him,
doesn't feel much like wisdom. Good story, though.
And thinking it over surely beats heck out of sitting around
making big idols out of one's problems. If you ever have trouble
distinguishing the queen of Sheba from Bathsheba, Solomon's mom
and his dad's first big transgression, just remember David saw
BATHsheba in her BATH. Careful: This trick won't work
in Hebrew, Greek, or Latin.

Things not lost today:
any weight, a tooth, my nerve.
Praise the plus column.

But does the eagle, its branch-nest humming atop a dead spruce
with chirpy eaglets hankering for fish, herring or mackerel
so fresh it was swimming just minutes ago, until the big swoop,
too fast to be fell, snagged it from the full-moon flood tide,
ever give an eaglish thought to whether or not to leave them alone?
Come on; confess. If you're an eagle, you rank pretty high
on the shoreline food chain and don't worry much about ending up
as somebody's lunch. And who could manage to raid that nest,
weighing in at a metric ton, when adults usually guard it?
But one of the parents could up and die and then the survivor
would be in a bind, having to exit to bring home the mackerel
while junior's defenseless. Helpless. Endangered.

Yellow-haired boy   arms to the sky   in yellow fall light
chasing to catch   yellow leaves flying.

I remember saying

you will remember this.
Now I remember this.

So many mysteries, no wonder detective fiction
has been so delectable ever since Daniel, in defense of Susanna,
cross-examined witnesses, or Oedipus, insistent,
sent for the shepherd, or Scheherazade's *Three Apples* story.
Who can't admire Auguste Dupin, Sherlock Holmes, Hercule Poirot?
Or the great Chief Inspector, who cracked many cases
while fathering analysis? But Freud had his blind spots,
among them a mystery beyond solution, so of course he belittled
religion as illusion; our largest spirits have never believed
in the God he didn't believe in either. What a low bar:
diss the divine into trivial silliness and then call it silly.
Talk about illusion: ideas of God are childish
so God is childish and doesn't exist? What logic primer
did he find that in? Grow up. You've finally figured out
God's not Santa Claus, a school principal hot to suspend you,
or your personal short-order cook? Good for you. Congratulations.
How does it feel to graduate from kindergarten?
Hope you do as well in first grade. Easy, Cush.
Unemployment's high and there aren't any jobs for more Jeremiahs.

In my trilogy
of sky and shore, wind and sea,
this is volume three.

So many mysteries, no wonder some like detective fiction;
solutions comfort, especially when mysteries come
with a copious side order of brain-dicing pain. But others?
Others may find investigation too exhausting
and opt themselves out of intractable inquiry:
When did this happen? Who did this to you? What do you remember?
Maybe it's better to kill the day in bed, skip the medication,
say you've been robbed of a certain kind of life,
one that sadness doesn't disfigure and force underground
out of the light of others' attentions, out of the headlines,
the prizes, the raises, the perks of looking good or doing well.

Or maybe detection, even successful, doesn't diminish
the deficit of hopelessness, so why bother trying?
Maybe, could it be, hopelessness is ecstasy?

Red leaf in the road.
This place will shake my dust off.
Crickets effervesce.

Ecstasy. There's a subject that's lots more fun
than spending a morning in General District Court
with shoplifters, trespassers, fishers without licenses,
inmates in jumpsuits who hobble to the bench in shackles
where the clean-cut judge, who doesn't sound judgmental,
denies them bond for risk of flight. Ecstasy. Much better
but in its way as complicated, variegated, unless you settle
for euphoria, bliss, exalted delight as adequate synonyms
and let it go at that, eager for the next installment, please.
But if the Greek means displacement from senses,
how can you settle for synonyms like those? So many ways
to end up displaced. The young man angry
at how his folks flubbed, ruined his life
from infancy on, isn't there ecstasy in the way he can't focus
on the simplest task or verbal exchange? Or how about sadness
his mother now feels, the majesty of her motherhood
suddenly spilled, unmoppable mess on linoleum floor?
Or ecstasy of fear as when someone says you jerk you scared me
shitlessly witless, or of boredom so bored one truly is bored
out of one's mind and into its boondocks. Ecstatic hatred,
ecstatic jealousy, ecstatic disgust, ecstatic confusion,
ecstatic embarrassment, ecstatic bereavement,
ecstatic compassion, ecstatic detachment, ecstatic obsession,
ecstatic stress in the ravishment of overwork. So much more
to ecstasy than pleasure, the back rub, hot bath, warm bed,
the fond folderol between your legs or someone else's.
When you get down to it, ultimate ecstasy,
super-deluxe, five-star vacation from the sensory grind,
wouldn't it be in the Grand Last Resort? Or if that's too glib,
wouldn't it be in whatever-they-call-it? Near-death experience?

(Well look at that: it's even got an acronym, NDE,
but surely the army could have done better, something more
like NEARTHEX, Sergeant, take those men and flank that NEARTHEX,
Yes sir, Lieutenant, except it sounds too much like narthex,
although come to think of it, the resemblance resonates;
when in doubt, reach for some Greek, parathanatosesthesia
perhaps, or perithanatosesthia, on the model of perimenopause,
pericarditis, peridontist, but not Perry Mason or Como,
and could yield the acronym PETE, suddenly changing
For Pete's Sake, or also possible, PETHE, which hip insiders
like us, who else, would pronounce PITH-ee when we apply
for grants to study the pithiest piths; where's my pill?)
But what do we do in the meanest of meantimes?
Here's the thing: there's no displacement from one's own senses
except through one's senses. If you're simply not interested,
skip this strophe and pick it up below; if you can't control
seizures, fits, or spells, you don't have a choice
and displacement will come, willy-nilly, sally-tally,
holly-folly, so good luck to you; if you're receptive
and in the market for a nice starter ecstasy, choose a sense
and then overload it, or bring it to the brink
of such overloading. Eyesight failing? Touch unavailable,
other than your own? Smell a little dull,
thanks to allergies or sinus infection?
Worried that taste will lead to gluttony and put on pounds?
Here's the good news. Words: organic, low-fat, gluten-free
and whether you're deaf or pretending to be,
they're all dressed to shimmy that auditory ecstasy.

Mates found or unfound,
birds shut their mouths and leave us
fall in songless woods.

yellow-haired boy   *electroconvulsive therapy*

arms to the sky   *severe depression*

in yellow fall light	*when psychotic*
chasing to catch	*refusing to eat*
yellow leaves flying	*thinking of committing*
yellow leaves flying	

Tough time lately
IDing a tree, its leaves turning red, first on the ridge
again this September, but even with a specimen branch
and field guide to common timber, one's small knowledge
of opposite simple leaves, edges smooth instead of toothed
and leafy veins concurred with edges, amounts to little
when it comes to pronouncing with confident conviction
the mystery tree a species of dogwood, which it might well be.
It's so much easier to say what it's not: buttonbush,
buffaloberry, the golden branch that must break off
for permission to visit, a visa for Hades.
Authorized Personnel Only. Hardhats Required. Passport, please.
I don't have a passport, but here's a branch I broke from a tree
I think might be a species of dogwood, although it differs
from the flowering ones that mostly go purple.
Are you kidding? You can't come down here with that.
Back up to the surface for you. No Admittance. Access Denied.
I know, I'm sorry, I thought it was just descent from the ridge,
maybe thirteen hundred back down to seven,
which is where I live if you call this living,
but I must have gone wrong, taken a bad turn,
since here I am, now flying stand-by, on Air Katabasis.
Well, as long as you're down here, let's see who's around.
No thanks. Little as I like what's up up there,
I can't handle it down here. Not so fast, pal;
somebody's recognized you; we got rules against rudeness.
Who is it? Over there. Tall, a little stooped,
orangish tonsure below a dapper hat. No, it can't be.

That you, Archie? *I'm at fifty Octobery.* Younger than I am
when we met. *How you getting along up there?*
Tough time lately. *Still writing?* Still writing.
Then what's the trouble? Hard to say. *Ease up; enjamb
more; let it all mosey.* It's not that. *What then?*
A yellow-haired boy. *Oh that.* Yes that. *I do
the ones I love no good.* Yes that: *there are those whom to lose
soaks direction out of the tree boughs.* That too.
You still got the letters I wrote? Got 'em right here:
*if treated obsessively it becomes obsessively important,
whereas, in fact, a good many things are important,
including the love between poets. Fight free
to the true spirit—.* Twenty-one when I opened that.
I treasure the knowledge of you. His age now. *I treasure
the knowledge of you.* Last thing you wrote me
twenty-one later. *Look me up when you're down here
for good; sign the guest book.*
I treasure the knowledge of you

A favorite cow,
calf-bereft, loudly out-lows
a bellowing bull.

Move forward move forward, but it's hard to know
where forward is down here, now a shore, a rocky stretch,
this bitch of a beach where urchins and barnacles
can slice the shoeless and ocean's so cold
heads hurt, privates burn, but no swimming like it
for a saline facial, a salty rubdown that sloughs dead cells
and when you get out in a fresh west wind it makes your skin feel
as if you'd taken communion on the outside: thus spake
the shivering imp, yellow-haired elf, blue eyes and goose bumps,
laughing tongue of laughing fire. Not every day
includes eagle-sighting or should, if it's special
and meant to stay so; not every place, no matter how real
the health it restores, the spirit it resuscitates,
or how thin the membrane between its trees and sacred emanations

is more than real estate in someone's eyes. One owner dies,
one survives, wants to sell, and just like that
it's gone, though still on the tax map and under surveillance
by satellites taking the very long view, gone, gone,
and if you're kin, even if distant, to airborne Antaeus
and needed your feet firmly on that ground or your face
in that water or your eyes on that eagle, then my poor friend,
you're one step closer, one giant's stride closer,
to being gone too. The Greeks got it wrong:
Mnemosyne's queen of the overstuffed underworld
where places go to be with people.

Been flipped the finger?
Only a prosodist can
give you the dactyl.

Can't move forward? At least change the scene,
eight straight days of some kind of rain, so heavy muggy
pages curl, covers warp, slime molds and fungi
erupt in the woods now studded with puffballs, inkhorns,
fatal Amanitas, one little bite of a Panther Amanita,
four-inch Death Cap, Destroying Angel, you don't feel a thing
for ten full hours, maybe more, but then it's too late
for puking to help or any kind of drug, but the great thing is
your change of scene, you nailed it cold, the underworld express
without all the hassle, delays, cancellations, long lines
at security, no room for your carry-on, the seat in front of you
smack in your face across the Atlantic or worse the Pacific,
while back upstairs in the light and air
the surface you rippled when you ate the wrong mushroom,
was it by accident, smoothes over fast and very best of all
it doesn't cost a thing. What a great deal but a tad extreme
for some mobilizers, who'd rather zip off to Europe instead,
London, Madrid, Paris, or Prague, whoopee, la-di-da,
welcome to Europe where thirty-eight percent suffer from illness,
we're talking mental, insomnia, anxiety, dementia, depression,
so welcome to Europe, sit back, relax, enjoy the quick trip

out of the pan into third-degree burn
over ninety-percent of your transient body.

No problem so huge
it doesn't shrivel puny
from a moon's-eye view.

Everything triggers sadness.
That's what he said, eyes filling up, while stroking a dog's ear.
He's right. Of course. Who can argue if anything can
trigger anything, and it's only a matter of how light you set
the trigger resistance. If you're motion sick or morning sick
or sickly hungover, a big bowl of chowder can make you upchuck;
horny, enthralled, obsessed, or infatuated, even the breeze
can be deeply engorging. So it makes perfect sense
that the sadder you get the sadder it looks, the sadder it looks
the sadder you get. The next question is is sadness the rule,
joy the exception, the most trigger-happy a gated community
of neurobiologies wired for mania, while the trigger-woeful
inherit the landfill. Or does joy have a chance
to get half the pie? Desolation Consolation Desolation
Consolation, how much of one offsets the other?
Can one arrive where it all triggers joy
without drugs or booze or mental disorder?
Black clouds backlit with hip orange edges: last night's sunset,
which after a day of even more rain was looking mighty foxy.

Recession's no fun
for gums and economies.
Rough on hairlines, too.

If it all triggered joy, you could just think
of the names of newborns, the three most popular,
Jacob, Ethan, Michael, virile trochees strutting smartly
to the Hebrew Bible, but girls mix it up more, number one,
Isabella, also Hebrew, a form of Elizabeth but more Español,
then off to Greece with wise Sophia, as Emma rounds it out,

whole, universal, with Old High German. Especially for guys
the Bible hangs on, the top twenty-five still bringing in
Noah, Daniel, Joshua, Andrew, David, Matthew, Elijah,
James, Joseph, Gabriel, Benjamin, and Samuel, whereas the girls,
except for Ava, akin to Eve, Hannah, Leah, and a couple of others
such as Nevaeh, heaven's own palindrome, go for the hetero
-dox or -geneous. Must be something to it, but what?
Maybe boys' parents, even agnostics, cling to nostalgia
for something like Logos and hope that their angels,
named for an angel, an apostle, a prophet, won't break the law
unspeakably badly and might end up righteous. If that's not a laugh
to generate joy and perk up an underworld, try the old system:
open the book at random and point. I hereby name thee
Shaphan, Jeremiah twenty-six, and now quite possibly
unisex like Jayden or Brandon or Rory. Hurray for the epicene;
joy's hard in jails, especially gender ones.

Jupiter rising
over sadness set to set
still shines when joys rise.

In rutty routine randomness refreshes, here the name Shaphan,
there the coarse bulldozer roaring next door. Who doesn't love
a blue October day, top-shelf weather with leaves turning too;
who doesn't hate the mechanized grinding, continuous drilling
by some sadistic dentist, or is there a nervous system
so calm and evolved, a brain so remapped by meditative practice,
it hears the grating growl as purling susurration? Wait.
It stopped. Now don't you feel like a jerk for complaining?
Now don't you wish you'd left lamentation
up to the soul-crushed who really have earned it?
Boo-hoo, so you're banished from the land of the eagle,
boo-hoo, so he's sick inside his handsome head,
boo-hoo, you can't travel and leave him alone,
boo-hoo, you can't sleep, boo-hoo, your shoulder aches,
boo-hoo, there's no raise, boo-hoo, you're always older,
boo-hoo, so your work has suddenly come to nothing.

Time's up. Quiet's over. It started again. Back to the dozing
of overbearing bull, or should it be dosing, as in a big dose,
a really big dose, of endless-link treads tearing up air waves,
getting in gear to gouge out the day, the china shop of silence
or small sounds and whispers, crickets winding down, wasps,
breezed leaves, a white-throated sparrow on his way south.
Instead get the earplugs. And where is that book,
since my last train of thought done jumped off the track.
No, not the Bible. Already downed a good shot this morning,
Jeremiah, Paul, especially that Matthew, do not be anxious
how you are to speak or what you are to say
whenever trial comes and you're delivered up, wish all my lectio
could be as divina, now that eyesight's even more precious,
wish all our tax collectors could sing the same song
or that the same song were soundtrack instead
of bulldozer muzak shattering Sheol. Here's the book,
thick and black, let's play the game, open at random,
Thou art now in the vale of misery, in poverty, in agony,
in temptation; rest, eternity, happiness, immortality,
shall be thy reward, as Chrysostom pleads, if thou trust in God,
and keep thine innocency. Though 'tis ill with thee now,
'twill not be always so; a good hour may come upon a sudden;
expect a little. Yeehah, now we're talking, keep on trusting,
keep up that innocency, expect a little, and most of all
don't continue reading, *Yea, but this expectation*
is it which tortures me in the mean time; future hope
makes present hunger; whilst the grass grows,
the horse starves.

That mackerel sky.
How big would they have to be,
eagles to eat it?

But then, starving horse, along comes a day, one single day
when, lo and behold, medication works, or is it good weather?
Or maybe it's prayer, go ahead and smirk, whatever the cause,
he's got a little zip, the smile shines again, there is the sound

of his chuckle and singing. Expect a little? Receive a lot,
glory be, alleluia, don't you dare think ahead
or look up this drug, what it's meant for, what the side effects
of antipsychotics they designate atypical.

Before dawn, ladies,
Jupiter was ogling
passing Pleiades.

Superlative blue of optimal October, how can one born to you,
with yellow light for breast milk and red leaves for toys,
question joy's inoculation or say such a thing
as the universe hates me? Today is a birthday.
Tell the black tupelo, maroon in the field,
to glow when he passes. Make the clear sun
apply to his cheek an ache-easing compress.
Swaddle him up in southwest wind
that tousles trees and floats the hawk
while smelling of ginger. Today is a birthday.
Let him gaze at zebras in gazebos;
let him liberate leopards in jeopardy.
Help him be born; help this day bear him
and him bear this day.

is silence escape from noise or noise from silence
contemplation escape from action or action from contemplation
built environment from rubescent maple or rubescent maple
from downtown buildings crammed with self-promotion?

That's a blot on your escutcheon.

Rhomboid in the male, triangular in the female,
escutcheon meaning shield-like pattern of pubic haircoat
is medical lingo and doesn't appear in the dictionary
usually used here or in any of the household back-ups, so it helps
to have a doctor friend, although the doctor also says
escutcheon meaning shield-like pattern of pubic haircoat

doesn't appear on many crotches these days either,
at least among the young or not so young who maybe figure
a little shaving's cheaper than a tummy tuck
and could be more effective in getting business back.

That's a blot, your escutcheon.

is faith escape from skepticism or skepticism from faith?

If you put it on display,
anticipate assessment.

so that the people could not distinguish
the sound of the joyful shout from the sound of people's weeping

Of those whom thou gavest me I lost not one
in all those years on that cold water not one
I took in a boat I never lost one not one

but this morning he wasn't in bed or anywhere
did I lose him would I find him at midday on the mountain
where he'd gone up to end it under Jupiter?

three times this week dreams of the house
someone else is calling home

the only thing better than sunset at sea is sunrise at sea;
there's no night sky like night sky at sea

the deeper the faith, the deeper the skepticism;
the converse may not be true

poo-poo to honolulu

What if the universe really did hate us does hate us
What if they got it wrong and bumper stickers should read
God hates you What if the constant onslaught of omens

signs oracles revelations theophanies amounts to an overflowing
inbox of heavenly hate mail and the eagle in the spruce
really means you miserable abortion of a soul I hope they
diagnose you tomorrow with inoperable pancreatic cancer
or Jupiter rising at downtime setting at uptime really means
may a beam pulled out of your house impale you on a dunghill
or the rubescent maple in the full throes of its blood-flush
mean let dogs dine on your precious interior the one you tended
petted caressed primped and plumed the one you gazed upon
doted upon drooled over and trumpeted abroad without ceasing once
in or on your memoir Christmas letter résumé web page podcast
blog a word so ugly so onomatopoeia for vomiting it makes
perfect sense where is she she's in the bathroom blogging
up her insights I'm so sorry I blogged all over your lap
oh no someone else announcing the substantial impact she's had
on American poetry these last thirty years I think
I'm going to blog What if this is really the way it is
What if he's right the universe does hate him and the medication
that could produce confusion fainting spells irregular heartbeat
frequent need to urinate stiffness spasms trembling constipation
sexual impairment sleeping impairment weight gain is nothing
but sugar-coating on the hate a rose-colored contact lens
for each blue eye so he sees the leaves as they let go
into the whirling wind sees and says let go let go
it will be all right the wind will lift me sail me up
and over this troubled time these troublesome times up and over
up and over until it's all over?

"I've fallen below the level of presentableness."

Give us a sign. But who needs a sign with signs and headlines
in such abundance, as in an airport: THE WORD FOREIGN
IS LOSING ITS MEANING. Really? What's the latest salary
of the genius who generated that tour de force,
expense account, retirement package, favorite hotel
in downtown Hong Kong? Does he or she stroll
with black designer roller-bag and matching laptop case

through this treeless, breezeless oasis on the way to a drink,
bourbon in business class, look up, and think
I wrote that one all by myself. Well, not quite myself;
I had a team on that campaign but remember the meeting,
time zones away, when the rhythm just came, who knows from where,
Is Losing Its Meaning Is Losing Its Meaning, *and when I shouted*
out loud to the board, we knew we had a winner
for the xenophobe market. Poor foreign. You're out of a job
if everything's domesticated, housebroken, tamed.
Nothing left alien, uncanny, exotic?
And all you meant was *out of doors.*

Praise the inventor
of headlights opalescing
dirty-blond fox fur.

Even if one's a steerage-class peon, courting blood clots
in a small middle seat on an overnight long-haul
back from the underworld, it's still good to read
the financial page of a decorous newspaper, if only to escape
aggressive alliteration in the hectoring headlines
of your typical tabloid, especially its sports pages,
but also because, even for investors only in invisibles,
financial headlines pay spiritual dividends. Consider:
FINDING YIELD IN A LOW-RATE WORLD. Okay, okay,
an auditory audit aimed at eliminating erotics for the ear
might object to terminal consonance in *yield* and *world,*
but quibbles aside, isn't this all that Emerson's saying,
for just one example, and isn't this really the basic goal
of the spiritual portfolio, no matter how diversified
among thriving theisms, mono-, poly-, pan-, and a-?
Or how about this one: WHY VOLATILITY MAY BE HERE TO STAY.
No need to bother reading the article; enough to know
tranquility gone AWOL in transactions with the world
isn't afflicting you alone, enough to grasp if peace and quiet
are high on your list, you'd better learn to grow your own
when they can't be imported. Five dismal days

of unbroken darkness, and then, with November,
he suddenly looked up. Today's a Thursday, Thursday the third,
the sky mostly sunny, highs in the 60s, lots of trees leaved.
But the last two months, his Thursdays go bad.

Aquila Jovis,
the eagle of Jupiter,
was golden, not bald.

It was and is not and is to come. How could he know,
John in the cups of Patmos apocalypse, that the beat of the beast
with seven heads and ten horns and a woman on its scarlet back
is the beat of the beast in a head so distressed?
Yesterday it was, unshakable shadow hooding his face
as if before hanging, but is not today because, who knows,
the angle of the sunset cuts more sharply or he dreams a dream
that leaves a good taste or some small short in neurotransmission
suddenly connects and power's restored, the juice resumes flowing
until it comes again, the reliable beast, repetitive bastard.
Have mercy, Master; my child's possessed, severely possessed
by a most severe demon. Nothing's changed. Two thousand years
and still the parents of offspring afflicted beseech and believe
in very little else. And can one blame a young man for hunting
escape from unbearables when the first day for muzzle-loaders
finds, yes it's true, his old father straying up toward the deer,
just before dusk, chancing an accident?

The light bleeds away.
November's the hemorrhage.
Three minutes each day.

Last stripe of afterglow in clear, cloudless sky
goes to ROY on the spectrum, while to the naked eye
for the first time tonight a new face in town
offsets austerity, the recent cutbacks handed down
and more light laid off: Venus returned from celestial sabbatical
spent behind the sun, its curtain drawn on her boudoir

these last eight months, but now she's back starring, however dim
compared to Jupiter, his maximum magnitude her eastern opposite
(somebody check: was he this big in 4 B.C.?), but bright enough
to outlast winter, exhaust its cold lechery, and rise refreshed
up through midspring. Bright enough. Bright enough.
As is the moon, three days from full, a screech owl trilling,
the white-throated sparrow's password at dusk, deer in the road,
three tails visible. This is enough. Or could be enough.
But not for him, along for the walk.

New tongues build your brain:
bird slang, colloquial breeze,
the phrasings of rain.

Most days one wakes parallel to the floor, overnight long-hauls
afflictive exceptions, but whether one's supine, all laid out
like Tutankhamun's gold sarcophagus or one of those knights
in dim Norman churches, hands chest-folded (my preferred mode),
or prone to sleep prone or hugging soft pillow, fetally balled,
the first roaring Rubicon yawns to be crossed: how does one get
from parallel to perpendicular? What's the carrot, goad, or spur
to drop that last dream, shed the cocoon of cozy bedclothes,
and somehow levitate ninety tough degrees to, let's say,
a grimly dismal Melvillian morning, November rain ripping down
the last of the oak leaves, nothing ahead but the usual gruel?
And this from an optimist, an eager believer in eager believing,
a poster-boy morning person who doesn't drink coffee
or tee off with tea and doesn't wake starving without any food
or to bars across windows and automatic-weapons fire.
What's someone luckless expected to do, lonely, despairing,
constant heartache that's not metaphoric but chronic anxiety,
its snug anaconda squeezing him tighter with each exhalation?
Sleep's his relief. Waking him's cruel, so isn't it better
to sit there a while, stroke the short hair, kiss the sad head?

I lift up my eyes
for some help to the foothills

the Spanish call skirts.

Thank goodness we're small and soon leave the earth
to much grander motions. Why care? Why try? Why bother
with a sabbath day you have to work hard to keep half-holy?
As long as we're resting, then let us start resting
from commandment number four, even though Mosheh,
drawn from the water (think no one's left for you to admire?
refresh yourself on Shiphrah and Puah), claimed it ranks higher
than later commandments that keep lawyers billing. It's simple really:
no sabbath, no rest of any deep kind; no rest, no distance
from the funhouse of feelings addiction to busyness
can make you think real; no distance from feelings, no chance
for your ashes to start to reheat, your juices regenerate,
your punctured lungs fill with fresh second wind
only true apathy gives mouth to mouth. We're talking
true apathy, as Stoics conceived it there in their portico,
not the kind now that endangers surprise and most curiosity,
but the bona fide kind that fires the drama jack king or queen
for magnification of minor emotion. Sure, feel sad
and then feel free to share that sadness with someone who cares
or wants to appear to, but then take a shot at letting it drop
and don't say you're dying unless it's high time to shop for a coffin.
If it is, speak the word, and we're off to the undertaker,
but if not, try transmuting sadness to askesis, lead into light,
rather than ass-kissing into high status they may not have earned
your ambient blues. Given a chance, sadness makes ascetic,
draining the appetites of erstwhile pleasures. Movies magazines
booze and most food can suddenly seem cumbersome, ditto the news
or keeping up with the latest buzz, the one going viral,
as if a virus were a plus. Pare things down. Bask in basics,
cool water, dark bread, weather, the sky; if it's available,
long-standing friendship simplified by trial into true trust.
Sex is trickier and not often thought of respecting ascetics,
appearing at first to have nothing to do
with self-control, strict discipline, or renunciative regimen,
but maybe it does, or maybe it can, since what's more austere

than absolute nakedness and how can one deny oneself
any more fully than when one surrenders one's self to another?

Yes, ithyphallic
once upon a bygone time.
Now, iffy-phallic.

"I'm sorry to be a parasite."

Abnormal skull: *fenestra rotunda* and temporal bones
distinctly pronounced, cochlea coil unusually large,
temporal gyri impressions, inferior and fusiform,
suggesting marked development of opposing cerebral zones.
Was he born with this brain, or did practicing music
alter its architecture? Say yes to the former
and Prelude and Fugue in E-Flat Major might as well be Jupiter
for all the chance you'll ever get there, but yes to the latter
and suddenly it matters how hard you practice pale sky scales
on December's first day or listen to gasps and the comelier grunts
these lines keep whispering into your ear as they go on trying
to work closely with you to find the right rhythm
one hopes might result in phonemic satisfaction, mutual esteem,
inclination toward future encounters. Ready readers' radars
with signals enough, discrete and discreet, and soon sensitivity
gets cranked so high it takes fewer words to enter the kingdom.
See that closed door? Someone's behind it stoking the notes
for your delectation and what's more there's no need
to huff and puff and blow the house down or sing to the door
paraclausithyrons of your own composition, no call to wheedle
or bully it open because the composer's not what you want
so bad you can't swallow; it's the thing that's composed.
Can't trance to Bach's skull, even in a powdered wig.

Rangers on their rounds
carry tampons in their packs,
slip them into wounds.

Sustain a gross insult to one's self-importance

and slip into sulking, prodigious, sublime, getting passed over
for raises, promotion, the Hot Stuff Award so stoking resentment
that one soon warps bitter, bitchy, and hurtful when suddenly
there she blows, the Goldilocks planet, six hundred light years
off through gray sky, where given a watery greenhouse effect
life may be happening—this rainy instant—and under a sun
a quarter less luminous (same way it seems down here some days),
its years sliding by with seventy-five fewer evenings and nights
(give them November, January too, and maybe throw in,
at no extra cost, July's second half). Discoveries like these
put the cosmic beats-me of nescioquiddity into ascendancy,
and one doesn't need didactic reminders of how not to be
conformed to this earth. Conformed to this earth?
What can that mean, when superlative earthliness
is scoping out space, hunting for planets? What about there,
somewhere on Goldilocks: is somebody saying be not conformed
to Goldilocks also, and does sentience there likewise distinguish
between Goldilocks versions of earthly and earthy?
Be not conformed to the earthy? What else is worth it,
if Professor Ornithologist has figured it out and sexual choice
in birds has to do not with genetics but with a strong preference
for what's merely beautiful? It makes perfect sense:
the eagle's an aesthete and mating is art, since art is a form
of communication co-evolving with its evaluation
(here's where the footnote should go if there were one),
though skepticism jumps to say, Then art doesn't differ in any big way
from marketing or politics. Oh stuff a sock in it
and take a few seconds to ponder instead how Professor explains
the angry upheaval we had only yesterday: if mating is art,
your face was displaying its luminous plumage
of tears in low lamplight.

Prosopagnosia,
worse than color, snow, or night,
blindness to faces.

Old and Middle Kingdom well-to-do Egyptians
sailed for the underworld in coffins lined with spells,

Here I am sailing, crossing the sky, but not afraid
because of good deeds, and litigants in Ethiopia
used to sue in poetic form, plaintiff or defendant winning
based on how the form impressed. Even an Inuit has better charms
up in the Arctic, warm in her igloo, humming as she mends a parka
one to stop bleeding, one to catch fish, one to make something
too heavy light. But where in the atlas can you find this:
*Whenever you sing, / Whenever it's dawn, / The path of death /
Will never be gone.* It's not in any coffin yet, and no one's
won a lawsuit with it, and now that the sun's already set
in Greenland, Nord, two months ago, you're not going to see it
again for two more, no matter the charm you happen to choose
or how hard you say it. No, that one's by a little boy,
five years old, composed by a river. They scanned his brain
this past Tuesday, the right side fine, so good at music,
Whenever you sing Whenever you sing Whenever you sing,
the waves of the left all scrambled and choppy. No wonder
he can't function sometimes, make a list, remember to call;
no wonder when December darkens, as it did Tuesday
for two rainy inches, he won't wake or speak at all

Whenever it's dawn   *Will never be gone*

It's not complaining
when starling wings start grumbling;
it's murmuration.

Solstice minus nine but just minus three till sunset ticks up
that first minute later and comeback's begun, spring's on the way
through ice storms and snow drifts with summer on its tail.
I am the frostbite and the heat prostration. In my wind chill
is my sun stroke. Half a million minutes in a calendar year,
even the worst, and that's their leading lady, at this latitude,
four fifty-five, December sixteenth, the tourniquet's applied,
we won't bleed to death, this year at least, from equinox-slashed
blue wrists of sky, bow down, bow down in total adoration,
high beta waves completely released in trances of theta
gamboling with gamma, so check your agnosis back at the door.

For Ahab had a little vial . . . whose fleece was white as snow.
No, no, don't horse around. Ahab had a little vial
of soundings in his pocket, for *nostos* to Nantucket,
which must have gone down in the North Pacific with him,
now mixed profoundly with its benighted bottom. Ahab had
a little vial smaller than a junk-shop flacon
half-filled with sand from that extinguished beach
only the eagle keeps eyes on now. The sand looks like pepper
coarse-ground from granite by eons of ocean,
the master spice, and yet does it help, a keepsake like this?
Or is all the flavor now past enhancing, the taste of each day
best left to blandness so palates forget, don't go off riled?
Light may seep back, but some day that sand will get thrown away
by whoever cleans out this cluttered little room. Let it be
him.
    He.
        Won't be long now, compared to time needed
for grinding up sand. The Hunter has started
making an evening of ending this autumn
above the black ridge line.

PART 2

One of those things, if dead people miss, I surely won't miss whenever I'm
   dead:
how long is that list, even for those who happen to convince not only them-
   selves
but hosts of the gullible in credulous legions with acrobat acts of contortive
   denial,
which make Pollyanna sound gloomy as Eeyore, that Pope had it right
that it's right, whatever, because it exists, because it just is, full stop, no
   predicate,
despite the appearance of what could be wrong with, say, how you're treated,
the mate who beats, enslavers who trade in sexual chattel, a conscientious
   torturer
doing his best on a gray Monday morning, and Pope has a right to some
   consideration,
tubercular bones, wrong religious faith, so it's not as though he had it so carefree
he'd find himself in sympathy with Life-Is-Good bumper stickers.
A puzzling question: when does one go for righteous indignation, respon-
   sible protest,
legitimate grievance in the name of reform, and when does one opt for rap-
   tures of gratitude
in melting acquiescence transcending all critique? Surely the latter is what
   we'd like in bed,
both to inspire and once in a while enjoy, and no doubt what we'd like to
   have in our beds
has wider application for how we get on with getting it on with existing
   conditions.
Then there's the question of when it's expedient simply to vent so you don't
   have to fester
and sprout an ulcer or, worse, a cancer, versus when is it better to do that
   deep breathing
and forego naked rolling in the nettles of negativity. One of those things
I surely won't miss whenever I'm dead: the dentist, visits to, such costly
   emergency.

Get thee behind me,
things I sink my teeth into,
breaking another.

There's a woman in church, lost a son, drowned, when he was thirteen and
     twenty years ago
the day after tomorrow her husband to cancer (she's always surprised some-
     one remembers,
but it's only addiction to big anniversaries), and now she's more than four-
     score and one
and had a stroke but worked her way back and leads weekly Bible study for
     most of the girls
at the local county jail, in their black and white stripes, who completely
     revere her
and get out of jail and look her up and keep in touch, and two years ago she
     got, at last,
to visit the Holy Land, always her dream, and she reads and studies, takes
     advanced courses
and sometimes speaks in tongues, though few people know it and she doesn't
     make a show,
and whenever you ask her, How are you feeling? she always says, Thankful,
     and not in a way
that sickens you with goo, and she's not prudish, she likes a tall drink
and good red wine, especially at Easter after a Lent of no cutting corners,
     and she can get mad
at money-changers in the temple and sometimes upset when people strain
     gnats,
but she's living proof, Thankful is possible, not because money is suddenly
     abundant
and your progeny are happy and headline successes and you yourself wake
every blessed morning pulsing with health and eagerness to start, any old
     aardvark
could be thankful under those conditions, we're talking Thankful that some-
     how depends
on nasty adversity, griefs so depleting, the grinding down to nub-hood by
     unredeemed routine,
without which daffodils, the first dozen shoots, poking up in January mean
     something less.

Warm the earth enough
and soon we'll take the chill off
our dead underground.

Last day of January, so long, good riddance, better to break another tooth
than live on planet January, better to break them all and proceed at once to
    gumming bananas
the rest of one's days than spend them instead on chipping windshields,
    blowing raw nose,
sucking sticky lozenges for tickles in the throat, but if one hopes to break the
    cycle
of negative thinking and unwanted thoughts, then this is not the way to
    start,
badmouthing months that cheat on their seasons and smuggle for our enjoy-
    ment
near-record readings in comfy high sixties, sweater off, windows open,
    maybe even
a nap in the sun as vultures float over, just making sure, and down on the
    pond
five pairs of mallards mingle with geese, the green-headed males feeding the
    scene
a few crumbs of color, so tangy on the tongue of a long-fasted eye, thinking
    like this
promotes mental health, the kind that Saint Henry would certainly endorse,
living in each season, breathing its air, drinking its drink, eating its fruit
no matter how frozen, and cheerfully resigning oneself to its influence in-
    stead of always thinking
this is wrong and that is wrong and making fun of politicians or resenting
    the kid
who's texting while you talk to him, as soon as you start down that lane of
    thought
you're a goner, thrashing in bewilderment at such bad manners and what
    they betoken
of a spirit so narrowed by defining the earth in terms of what interests, dis-
    tracts, entertains
that any enlargement becomes unsustainable, if it requires a step toward the
    dead,
who can't step our way to help us comprehend, but the kid is so smug

he cannot imagine why someone would care about anything past or requir-
   ing exertion,
his cheap self-reliance successfully sold him by those who make the gadgets
to which he's enslaved, thinking like this won't get you anywhere except into
   bitterness,
and bitterness becomes the coldest of horrors that never lets go and refriger-
   ates the soul
into inner January shattering record lows, this sort of thinking enshrines
   unwanted thoughts,
adding yet more to one's persistent pantheon, most recently joined by one
   day discovering
the glossy black dog, so fit and strong and fast through the woods, lying
   down and chewing on
what turns out to be, on closer inspection, another canine's forepaw, severed,
maybe a fox's, maybe coyote's, maybe a pet's caught in a trap, toss up what's
   worst,
the prospect of a forest floor mined with unsprung traps, the slobbering
   pleasure
the dog clearly takes in cannibalizing his cousin, or the sickening handshake
of limp limb and soft pads in the grasp that takes the trophy away.

On chemo she said,
No one did anything great
while nauseated.

Take the glaciers, how they calve, gigundo chunks of turquoise face
one day splitting off and spilling, slow-motion, into saltwater, numbing,
of, say, Glacier Bay, the displacement blowing up a blast of spray and waves
enough to rock a cruise ship or swamp a kayak or incautious canoe that
   floated too close
to depth-charging waterspouts one doesn't have to be John Muir, suckled on
   Emerson
(whose Yosemite handlers wouldn't permit him to sleep under stars),
to swoon at in seizures of sublimity beatified. This is how the last year's
   been,
hefty slabs of erstwhile self just sloughing off and making fat splashes
the small things of Thursday continue to bob on. But maybe a self's not only
   fiction

but obsolete too, having emerged whenever you choose, ancient Egypt, clas-
    sical Greece,
during the Renaissance, it's now fading out, and speaking of self, like Whit-
    man or Dickinson,
is day-before-yesterday thrift-store nostalgia. Instead of a self in search of a soul
or kindred soul-mate, you now have a network of texters to text, private
    selves superseded
by inboxes brimming (voices of geese landing on the pond), the texter inter-
    textual
with tons of texters around the world, the Aussie you play chess with or
    Ruskie who shares
your love of film noir. Don't snicker, if you're not like this, and don't feel
    judged
if you happen to be. Maybe we've achieved Emerson's beatitude and crossed
    the bare common,
minus sloppy snow puddles in cloudy-sky twilight, our mean-ego selves
    finally emptied out
so currents of something can circulate through us, Being, Universal, in the
    lingo of Concord
but now social media and what's mediated, a feeling of fellowship and total
    togetherness,
unsundered communion, world without end, part and parcel of perfect part-
    ners, not only no need
for an old separate self but that old separate self a positive hindrance, a blem-
    ish, a flaw,
undissolved flour, a lump in the gravy. Sing it, sage yankee: spirits build houses
and beyond houses worlds and beyond worlds heavens, and now there's an
    app for it,
mi casa tu casa, mi mundo tu mundo, mi cielo tu cielo. Now that mine eyes
have seen this salvation, let me go, pretty please. But in peace, pretty please.
Slave manumission gave Simeon that formula. In peace was important. And
    it still is,
so if it ain't peaceful, then what say thou lettest thy unpeaceful servant
stick around forty days, see if the groundhog got it right this time.

Kindle a candle
in honor of anyone
purified today.

There's a guy who's had it with working for the state these last five years
     without any raise,
so he's quitting the public to run his own travel business, on line, low over-
     head,
and travel means bucks, especially cruises, which pay him good fees, but
     travel means also,
or meant in Old French, travail, which it was when those pilgrims started
     climbing
into the Pyrenees on the Way of Saint James toward rainy Santiago, the
     hardcore on knees
bloodied by cobblestones the last hundred yards, up cathedral steps,
homestretch of journeys to knock time off Purgatory, that last of the lay-
     overs,
and travail whispers torture, pain-inflicting instruments made of three stakes
brought you by the people who invented crucifixion, but things have
     changed,
now you can travel in swishy first-class, or if not you, you can see it, and
     knowing it's there
puts leg cramps and blood clots in comforting perspective as not ineluctable
but merely the symptoms of personal failure to hustle hard enough,
so except for jet lag and digestive confusion, travel's not bad and shimmers
     there beckoning
to the young with no jobs and the old who have finished and those in be-
     tween
who somehow get on by getting out of town at acceptable intervals.
A change of scene helps when nothing else changes, the overly familiar
exotically strange for a few precious days upon your return, or at least a few
     hours
of something like drunkenness, your commuting aglow with uncanny buzz,
ditto the grocery store where one can observe the colorful customs of native
     inhabitants,
maybe take a picture if no one gets offended, but for some there's no need to
     travel at all,
or not anymore, things they thought solid all turned to mush, a porridge so
     foreign
why bother paying for tickets to somewhere that isn't more distant
now that the son has died in his thirties, that lifelong love-link has finally
     rusted through,

your layoff has come or maybe a tumor with a different kind of pink slip
or betrayal so utter everywhere is exile. Averagely aging's a travel agent, too,
something done daily with devotion for decades, in firm belief of mighty
    purpose,
one day looks to others so quaint, something for the scrapbook forgotten on
    a shelf,
at which point many opt for turning crabby, anathematize ephemera,
lest they see ephemera comprehending them, or does one say a thousand thanks
for this undeserved upgrade, a window seat on a land unknown and never
    conceived of
where notes of the dove know nothing of mourning?

Know a drama queen
of ups and downs overdone?
Slip her Dramamine.

No wonder there's need to fantasize apocalypse, a cataclysm big enough
to get us off the hook, waking each day and soldiering on, upper lips rigid
or divorced from the lower in photogenic grimaces approximating grins,
whatever it takes to ward off a narrative of downward-trending tendency,
the bedtime story of sliding decline that makes sleeping tough on full-moony
    nights,
be what it may, my needs aren't met, my burdens aren't eased, my powers
    aren't sufficient
to attract and be attracted, satisfy and be satisfied, and that goes for spirit
as well as for body, maybe goes double in the most woeful cases, so lucky
    there's disaster,
the hovering prospect of humans deleted and my problems with them,
so many flavors and toppings to choose from for snuffing homo sapiens,
our weapons could do it, maybe a plague, there's always the climate
as long as it's climactic and doesn't drag out eventual extinction,
giving the living time to adapt and accommodate diminishment,
but the newest chef's special's a solar storm warning, sunspot activity re-
    ported on the rise,
that would do fine, corona mass ejection, the sun cuts one off, the biggest
    one ever,
and there we all are, crispy fried bacon, the whole turning earth a blue roast-
    ing spit,

what's great about that one, it can't be our fault, nothing we've done's faintly
     perceptible
five hundred light-seconds up in the sky, and as a nice bonus no one escapes,
no one, that's important for this fantasy, no need to ponder possibly surviving
to try to make the best of it, no one repenting, forgiving, improving, no one
     to envy
and secretly resent, no one left thirsting for ice-chipped compassion
some days he lets me place on his tongue.

Only a loser
would sound so defeatist
or an elitist

but what's an elitist, and who gets to be one when it's a bad word, a pejora-
     tive putdown
or synonym for clique, coterie, in-crowd exclusive and sniffingly snobby?
     Valentine's day,
cold-snap departing, Venus a spotlight in post-sunset west and closing the
     gap
twixt her and Jupiter, merely three fist-widths between them last evening,
     gibbous moon waning,
geese on the pond, nine at last count, one of them widowed or part of a
     triad, daffodils stalled,
morning sky gray. Are lovers elitist? What's more elite than will you be mine,
my selected superlative? What about the dying this very minute in hospice
     or hospital,
a hut or a car wreck, on a bare mattress or street paved with gunfire? Death's
     democratic,
clucks the cliché, but that can't be right. Somebody dying's suddenly above
     us,
exempt from our chores, no longer in service, a paradigm of privilege freed
     from the grind,
the ultimate aristocrat beyond condescending. Then take the crazy or psychi-
     cally stricken,
nothing Joe Blow or Man in the Street about someone who's suffering with
     bad basal ganglia,
serotonin receptors perhaps under-stimulated, resulting in thoughts, intru-
     sive, unwanted,

of violence or sex or sexual violence, which attack him like seizures and
    won't fade away
à la nightmares on waking. From his point of view what's more insipid
than unbroken intercourse with working and earning the food that needs
    cooking
and serving on dishes that later need washing? Compared to us masses
of payday pedestrians, he's elite, he's elect, one of those chosen and, marked,
    set aside
for special distress that makes up a class that couldn't care less who's hungry,
who's fed, who's got the money or best education. Compared to the leisure
of brains free to wreak unease on themselves, unhurried, unscheduled,
    what's the odd morning
spent watching vultures who coast by in play while once again asking

what the heck is this
metabolic disarray
that seems here to stay?

Out the kitchen window first open daffodil, tentative yellow-head sticking its
    neck out
to fence-sitting February, genus Narcissus, can't get away from him, family
    Amaryllis,
thank goodness a shepherdess, Daffadown Dilly, come munch on that bulb
    and maybe wake up
Elysium-blissful, eternally elite, surrounded by asphodel, which Dutch
    turned to daffodil.
Associate at this rate, past Wordsworth's sad couch, and soon caress every-
    thing
except the kitchen sink, but why not caress the kitchen sink too, what better
    place,
if you must be inside, to have it both ways and be outside also, assuming
    there's a window
opening on daffodils, hands in the suds but sight climbing up and through
    the bare woods
till soon the inward eye's back on the ridge, no dishes around, no daffodils
    either,
but maybe today a deer or a turkey, could see a fox or day-shifting owl or
    given a winter

so mercifully wimpy, with luck a rare bear, once saw coyotes but never a
    bobcat,
though they're up there too and can do you some harm, especially rabid, and
    if there's a quota
of those to be killed by some of the animals development's missed, that's a
    vocation
a few can fulfill, not with grand notions of sacrifice for others, but more like a tip
left for good service, thanks for the decades of letting me trespass, now you
    can eat me
and so cheat the funeral home, seems only fair, and perhaps I'd taste better
than dozens back home in town planting daffodils, which somewhere grow
    wild,
Grasmere I guess and elsewhere in Europe, also North Africa and apparently
    Asia,
but here they're just imports, good for the garden club, also the florists, who
    have to watch out
for daffodil itch, no kidding, it's true, because of the sap and all the Narcissus
can poison with lycorine, who needs more parable, so maybe there's still
    some wildness left
growling in the garden, but wildness is complicated and always needs more
    thinking
even by Thoreau, who, yes, is my hero, though he's a touch fussy when it
    came to the animals
or maybe just a dope who wrote better sentences, except for one ending
"but the traveler can lie down in the woods at night almost anywhere in
    North America
without fear of wild beasts." Henry, come on man, two last year in Yellow-
    stone alone
done in by brown bears, then you've got wolves making a comeback and also
    the mountain lion,
who savors small children. But what he got right is wildness lives, beyond
    the Sierra Club,
in people as well, in lovers' *awful ferity* (don't think he's sexy? you could read
    more closely)
and also in killers, though he doesn't say so, but who needs a wilderness or
    any preservation
when yesterday the prosecutor, resting his case, rich kid allegedly did in his
    girlfriend,

left to the jury, allegedly till Friday, what kind of killing, and that's just down-
town
in the small courthouse surrounded by daffodils and lots of big news trucks.
If no news is good news, why watch the news? There. All dishes done
and done without thinking

does no news from him,
poplars sprouting robin leaves,
mean bad news again?

Fricking fickle February. No sooner out than that daffodil bought it
under six inches of weighty wet snow, first of the winter and already melted
enough to reveal the yellow head down. Dead head confirming declensionist
narratives,
as in we'll all live unhappily ever after, sooner or later, but not ever after
and maybe not all of us, though lots of us will? Or is it just bed head (I get
that bad),
the snow having ruffled its premature petals, which soon will rebound and
all will be well,
the lumps one has taken first-cousins of those in flocculent soil, what a great
word
and what a great thing for soil to be, its lumps the sure signs of ongoing
health,
plenty of airflow around the loose aggregates, waterflow too, good for the
plant roots,
flocculation, let it thrive, not only in soil but also in cheese curds and beer
fermentation,
flocculent clouds, fluffily woolly, and flocculent galaxies, patchy, discontinu-
ous
in how their arms spiral, snow could be flocculent, couldn't it also? yesterday
morning
flocculent clods plopping off branches, trailing behind them sun-gauzy
dustfalls,
and sentences too, the flocculent ones with moments of tufting to slow our
attention
to pools of adhering before the next runoff. This is the way to think of one's
lumps,
or could be the way to take a few more, which won't keep us waiting,

but always the test of any such theory is whether you'd try it on someone in
    jail,
the kid across town alone in his cell, awaiting his sentence, which he'll get
    tomorrow,
also Ash Wednesday, the big Lent for him, no forty days just giving up choco-
    late
and cheating on Sundays, but probably years on top of the two he's already
    spent
fasting from wind, from laughter, from sky, Mars out at night now, just be-
    fore bedtime
but he'll never know it, not with his own eyes. So what do you say to him
    about lumps?
You gave her some, and she died of those, though no one knows how or can
    know for certain,
so now you take yours, which won't be so bad, inmates have friends and also
    TV,
and if you behave, you may get a job, picking up trash on days the sun shines,
and when you get out, as likely you will, maybe your life will be something
    larger
than too much dough and too much booze and beating people up in ongoing
    anger?
Punishment's hard; penitence too. Tough to think of malefactors getting off
    scot free,
but just as tough, at least for some, to think on fifty or sixty more years of
    nothing
except remorse and reviling oneself. Talk about hell; he's deep there already,
no need to wait and see if it's true, but what should we do? Can we do any-
    thing?
Should we give discounts based on contrition? Punch me in the eye and
    laugh,
you die, but punch me in the eye and cry for what you've done, I cut you
    slack,
though my eye's just as black. Seems an odd system and basically based on
hurting another as he has hurt me, who hurts him back, his conscience or I,
of lesser importance than that he hurts somehow, but what if his hurting
is what made him hurt me at first to begin with?

Eat up, Fat Tuesday,

and don't count the calories.
Slimming is coming.

Now that it's Lent, so long to seconds, except for a few, second base maybe
        (what was her name,
back in eighth grade?) and surely second fiddle (not hard to play, once you
        learn how);
lots of second childhood, though now it's dementia, prize for longevity and
        not quite as cute;
the second commandment, abstracting divinity, guaranteed idolatry would
        seek other forms,
but some found a loophole in human incarnation and now live in hope of its
        second coming;
second thoughts, second guesses take up the brain waves, more than their
        share, then again
maybe not; some people's houses have second stories, not high enough to die
        jumping out of;
buy someone's wristwatch, a second-hand second hand; and don't forget the
        second person
is your chance to play. Is there a second? Thank goodness for order. Read
        Robert's Rules
when at loose ends, a brigadier general, served in the Pig War, wrote his
        pocket manual
after a meeting, churchful of Baptists. The chair recognizes. Reconsideration?
So moved, Madam Speaker, lest we overlook second-degree burns, red with
        clear blisters,
or second-degree murder, which the jury gave him. With twenty-six years.
        Twenty-six years
may not amount to prison for life, he'd only be fifty the day he walks out, but
        they could do fine
for ringing down his parents' curtains. And maybe also mine. Such fabulous
        phobias,
chromatophobia, chionophobia, bromidrophobia, color, snow, b.o., e.g., but
        not one for death.
Why leave it out? Because it's endemic and so isn't aberrant? Maybe so,
        maybe so,
but timor mortis conturbat me needn't be a personal refrain simply because
        one likes statistics:

how many more droughts, hurricanes, blizzards? how many more eagles can
   one hope to see?
bears or whales, full eclipses, shooting stars? how many more presidents yet
   to vote for
(not everyone finds a low number lamentable) and how many passports
still to apply for? dogs to put down? used cars to dicker over? Must be about
   time
to shingle the roof again, having torn off the two layers there, and if one
   should choose
thirty-year shingles, any bad plywood also replaced, the roof overhead one
   likes to have
won't need reroofing again in this lifetime. The first of the lasts. Today's the
   first day
sunset's at six. Daffodil's down still, yellow head hanging, but abundant
   developments
egg on toward optimism. Six o'clock sunset means seventeen days till we can
   spring forward,
so don't abandon hope, you who enter there, prison guards are people too,
   you still have a soul
and Saul also killed. Plenty of time to catch divine breath, find second wind.

Across the live fence
a young black bull bellies up
to a heifer's rump.

Daffodil's up again, rebounded yesterday, today it's just strutting, thumbing
   its trumpet
at six skimpy inches, that your best shot, colleagues more cautious finally
   show faces,
a maverick like that deserves a good nickname, Friedrich, no, Fred, Ni-
   etzsche's too formal,
possibly Henry, resisted Sunday's snowstorm, but shortened to Hank
or maybe go with Waldo, who lasted out his share of lumps, wife's death,
   brother's death,
son's death, Margaret's death, Hank's death, burning of his house, but he
   kept at it,
kept the head up, kept the soul darting, never said the hell with this, I'm
   ready to go,

or never wrote it down, courage, man, that's what it is, raw, dogged courage
to rise every day into tragic trajectory, if not yours or not how you see it,
then that of the person shuffling next to you, head down, stare blank, some-
thing big missing,
drinkable water, nourishing food, a place to live, dawn without pain, one
single friend,
affectionate touch, a job that pays enough to live as something other than
somebody's slave,
the list is long, the list of ills we rack up collectively, and, sure, we make it
worse and longer
with all our complaining, our self-pity blubbering, our failure to focus on
bounty at hand,
but you can't laugh away a tumor in the rectum or a skinny fixed income
with steady inflation
and three square meals of cat food in your future, these ills are real and will
make demands
on whatever you've got in the way of philosophy, homespun or book-learned,
your private concoction of pessimism, optimism, stoicism, hedonism, skepti-
cism, nihilism,
so you best get it brewing, but that's assuming your mind has the chops even
to get you
that far along, since one mental illness or emotional distress, neurosis, psy-
chosis, SAD or PMS,
post-partum depression, eating disorder, anxiety disorder, -mania, -philia,
take your own pick,
you know the tune, we haven't got all day, and suddenly, siblings, that frisky
philosophy,
it's in the big trash bin. At least sky is free. Not all can see it, the blind, for
instance,
or someone in jail segregated solitary, and those who can see it, not all see it
well,
people in cities who live in the light slums and rarely glimpse stars or naked-
eye planets,
but up there they are, no one's figured out yet how he can charge for them,
Venus and Jupiter a fist-width apart, and waxing moon hanging right over
top
as in the east, opposite, rising Mars watches, roughly the hue of a female
cardinal.

True, there's private property even in the sky, satellites and space stations, all
    kinds of aircraft
grooving their ruts, and some day, you wait, there will be war involving the
    moon,
if not upon it then certainly about it, who gets to be there with what type of
    weapon,
but for now not a fence or trespassing sign, the eye free to roam and with it
    the spirit
in need of a lift or maybe a break from indoor commitment.

Leap Day tomorrow
keeps Gregory's calendar
in step with the sun.

Things cost a lot and more every day, so if your employer's committed to
    raises
having nothing to do with what living costs and everything to do with what
    he can get from you,
how hard you work could always be harder, your choice is simple, you can
    work harder
and harder and harder in hope that your effort will somehow be noticed by
    people in charge
of most of your soul and most of your time, if one can split them, or start to
    wise up
to how competition means some suck the mop and get set to suck while
    finding the free stuff
here to enjoy and not just enjoy but feed on and live by, like the free sky even
    when cloudy
or here's a great bargain, eavesdropping, gratis, simply for listening, not as in
    phone-tapping
or planting a bug, but just in the street as people pass by, two girls power-
    walking off to a gym,
parallel pony-tails bleached the same blonde, in lively discussion of spandex
    and tank-tops,
when suddenly one says, "I really like love it," and, lo, there it is, the burning
    bush flickering,
like-love, it's perfect, the name for affection, attraction, some ardor but none
    of it so deep

one can't change the channel or click a new screen, just enough love to keep
the day perky,
cheerful, and upbeat, a fun, breezy way to sign off on messages, Like-Love,
Francesca,
but not the hard love fusion is made of, love that's a calling, amidst their
insistence,
away from one's interests and brooks no distraction, no loss of eye contact,
that has little use
for languid lukewarmth and may guarantee, when raises arise, performance
suffers elsewhere.
Maybe both girls know much of such love, like your employer. Judgment,
suspend it.
Who knows enough to say in the long run like-love's not better for running a
country?
If hard love's your lot, you're on your own, assembly required, consolation
not included,
so don't ask for any and don't get seduced by treasure in heaven, love of
which breeds
just as much avarice. Consider hand-sanitizer, in lieu of the lilies, which
boasts that it kills
ninety-nine point ninety-nine percent of bacteria common to households,
pretty impressive,
rate it triple-A, give it a raise, but there's still one one-hundredth that some-
how gets through
and that's the hard love or in some people faith, which won't go away and
isn't for everyone.

Some days it hinges,
how to last another month,
on high cardinal song.

Seven more inches pounced on this morning during a run, make that a trudge,
third gear at best but on the tough hills no more than second, such a slow
crawl,
out to the doctor, shoveling his lot, for annual physical, not as much fun as it
once used to be,
but he likes to talk and gladly to teach the comic economy of this fleshly
house,

the present embodiment and permanent address until the next move, no
   mail forwarded,
no current occupant, as far as we know, once the first owner has broken up
   camp,
palpation for instance, abdomen bared to flakes out the window, what one is
   looking for
is nothing to feel, don't want that spleen enlarging with anger, crowding
   stage left,
while there to stage right let's keep the liver tucked under the rib cage, not
   let our prayers
and forms of obeisance to Lord Dionysus give Zeus's eagle lots more to snack on,
punishment for uppity, but that looks unlikely around here these days,
not many defying on others' behalf, risking the outrage, befriending the puny
when puniness affronts the new business model, possibly because sometimes
   we need
help from the powerful, two county cops, young guys with muscles, really
   strong backs
and really strong legs, who don't need to bother with annual physicals, jellied
   gloved finger
up the back alley, the two of them pushing, exerting their force against the
   front tire
of a little black car now down to first, to keep it from ditching, blocking
   things up
on a thin rural road, already clogged with fluffy March snow, another car
   flipped
inside the white tunnel bowing trees make, it's called sugar snow where
   maple sap's rising
to stacks of hot pancakes lathered in butter, which these guys can eat and
   should before shifts
that wholly consist of helping us out, keeping things moving in adverse
   conditions,
but one day that butter belongs to the past, for many a waistline, let alone
   artery,
and as for the future, that's the big question, the master prognosis, how long
   have I got
to keep this up, making an effort to keep finding reasons to keep the house up
when after the blood work and sphygmomanometer, after the chest hair

shaved for electrodes and heartbeat stalagmites rising on graph paper,
moonlight on snow's not reason enough.

Give me a reason,
with thawing in the down spout,
one needs a reason.

Some days it comforts to think of extinction, sorry, that was Jay
calling to say five hundred should do it, coolant flush, transmission fluid,
    fuel induction
before the new spark plugs to help with good mileage, as power diminishes,
    if only
one could be a little black car, up on the lift for ninety thousand service or its
    equivalent
in late middle age, whenever that starts, who knows anymore, ream out the
    arteries,
tune up the ticker, tighten the screws events have worked loose, whatever is
    sending
you round the bend, love or lack of, marriage or lack of, children or lack of,
employment or lack of, money or lack of (one can have too much, like
    booze),
addiction or illness, skip the distinctions, mental from physical, or maybe
    you suffer
from too much compassion and can't hear the news without a quick slip into
    full catatonia
or too much indignation and can't hear the news without coming close to
    stroking right out
in seizures of fury, sorry, that was the Democrats, or was it Republicans, dun-
    ning for dough,
or maybe these troubles to you would be luxuries, silken distresses, com-
    pared to a life
of grains and legumes, contaminated water consumed in a hut or building-
    scrap shanty
and that's before war or famine in drought, sorry, that was Out of Area, didn't
    pick up
but possibly should have and suddenly heard Ghana, out in the country, or a
    slum in Chennai

or township near Cape Town, a week ago snow, today it hits eighty, and
     maybe a voice
that simply says Help, a softy, gaspy whisper, or maybe a voice, light-plump
     and comforting,
that says yes indeed, some days it helps to think of extinction, not piecemeal
     by species,
great auk, dodo, Irish deer, Tasmanian tiger, but massive extinctions, like the
     big five,
Permian the worst, back a quarter-billion, ninety-five percent of animal spe-
     cies known
wiped out like that, or the best, if you think of it as something like a power
     wash
the sun gives the earth every few million, scrubs her clean, hoses her down,
routine maintenance performed on schedule, nothing to fear, no matter your
     species,
though self-importance could take a hit, stock in your legacy subject to sell-off,
and if you consider humans the summit, you might get bummed out, but
     think of a species
five or ten million off in the future, whatever it takes for animal recovery
from the next big extinction some think we're into, a species that views our
     fossils and bones
in museums with wonder as we a T-rex, perhaps in displays, interactive,
     dimly lit,
that reconstruct our flesh and show off our asses better than they ever
     looked,
how they'll marvel and maybe recoil and think beyond mystery, having
     solved it,
the bogus split, religion from science, to them no difference, the Supreme
     Presumed
blessing all data with divine verifiables, nothing more to test, experiments
     completed,
nothing to believe, revelations completed, they'll look at us and know our
     place
in the terrestrial story and yet know nothing about any one of us, whom she
     loved,
what he worried about, the long hours spent in vigil by the phone, awaiting
     a call
from someone much younger, stricken again

(Winter is over,
periwinkle everywhere.
The snakes are awake.)

but then, the next day, up off the couch, doing much better. Is it the moon
that takes him down monthly, not much choice for some fertile females, but
    anything up there
strong enough to bleed them while raising the tides must have some power
over others too, no matter how well we insulate against it, earthbound rou-
    tines
our mightiest bulwarks, trundling the trash down yesterday morning, still
    before dawn,
thanks to the annual setback for sunrise, and there it awaits, rheostat high
low in the south and gibbously waning but shining robust despite the dimin-
    ishment,
close to Antares, earning its name, opposite Mars, ahead in the west and last
    night on show
though nothing like them, Venus and Jupiter, down to thumb's width soon
    after sunset,
could be two eyes, a snakebite, a colon, or maybe an umlaut, the latter two
    tilted,
though she's now the brighter, Cythera to Ez in his thin tent at Pisa,
but here she's just Venus, not only brighter but lately on top, how nice for
    her, and after today
moving away, the space between growing, the spectacle peaked, whatever
    they do,
electromagnetic, to our touchy fields having been done, leaving us under
some other influence stronger than theirs, or soon to be so as they move
    apart,
so you take a breath test and come away clean, so you take a urine test and
    nothing shows up,
whatever you're doing you're under the influence, if not of the moonshine
that comes in a jar then under the kind that comes in the eye and in through
    the pores
and comes and comes and keeps on coming, even when shining on some-
    where in China,
beware the March ides, i.e., today, or don't give a hoot, it's really up to you,
have it your way, see if I care whether you're stabbed twenty-three times,

nice place, Rome's Senate, or thirty-three in Shakespeare, it's all the same to
    me,
your good days, your bad days, your ups, your downs, your allergy analogy,
your pseudo-sadism, whether or not you can bolster a lobster, you're under
    the influence
of something unseen, sound waves for sure, lapping the eardrum, but also
    the microwaves,
cell phones and cordless ones, towers, antennae, radar and satellites, com-
    puters, TVs,
we're all mice in this experiment, there is no control group, everyone's ir-
    radiated,
children most vulnerable, their skulls still thinner, their cells still dividing,
so what'll it be, something reproductive, or make it the cardiac, no, not for you,
you want the best, headaches, sleep problems, memory loss, attention disorder,
as long as it's neurological, but all shall be well, and all shall be well,
all manner of things, even these, shall be well.

Psychic S.O.S.?
Try etheric surgery;
your fields are a mess.

First day of spring and one of Picasso's Avignon damsels steps from his canvas
onto thronged sidewalk, not in a Fang mask, that African phase, but with
    half her face
a port winy birthmark, its side, the left, a little bit saggy, as after a stroke, her
    left upper lip
swollen and drooping, while starboard side's typical of a young healthy
    woman
not in spring uniform of short shorts and flipflops, not on her cell phone or
    texting while walking
or wired with earbuds, auto-erauditory, her parents must cherish her, sib-
    lings and friends,
but she'll never win Miss Dogwood Parade or Forsythia Queen and chances
    are low
she'll land many perks prettiness brings young female westerners, even post-
    feminist,
drinks and meals they never pay for, seats given up on buses by old guys,
    speeding tickets

waived by avuncular cops, the choice over others to be the receptionist for
   no real reason
other than matching our canons of beauty, which takes work, no question,
but some get disqualified before the race starts, what are they left with,
   what's in it for them,
there has to be something to hold her head up through yet another day of
   fascinating people,
who don't look away, with a shot of the hideous, slopping straight through
   the muck of their pity
she'd rather not have and maybe resents, there has to be something, fairness
   requires it,
maybe she's a genius in nuclear engineering, has a great job, Department of
   Defense,
working on battleships, our most secret subs, or concert violinist on grand
   world tour,
since childhood a tennis star, now turning pro, or if not things she does then
   certainly her soul
is way above average, surely it must be, her defect begetting a larger defection
from the vainest inanities so many wreck on, that's it, her soul, perfected by
   disfigurement
to loving enlightenment, nonstop to heaven, or if she's a Buddhist, release
   from rebirth
and all forms of suffering, fairness requires somehow she's compensated, this
   is the law
Emerson believed in, a minus here means a plus there, what's more attrac-
   tive
than having it balance, all even stephen, nobody screwed, not in the long run
or in the big picture, sub specie aeternitatis, maybe it's true, Emerson's right,
but maybe it's hogwash, fairness a lullaby some sing themselves, while she's
   sad and lonely,
not very bright, petty and selfish, long ago hopeless, each day a desert never
   in bloom,
what then, now what, no means of redress, not only not a winner but in fact
   a big loser
and not so remarkable even in her losing, just one of the mass of those who
   don't win,
no matter how many awards we invent, one can get sick of the topmost
   percentile,

whether in appearance, achievement, or affluence, not out of envy or sour
    grapes sweet teeth
but just because the top is a small place to be, it's narrow up there and way
    claustrophobic
and not a good view in spite of the altitude, the summit socked in with pic-
    tures of itself,
it's hard to stay satisfied, so self-satisfaction must be a big job, take up one's time
and most of one's attention, it's better down here, the corset less tight,
easier to breathe, lots of good company.

First it's literal.
Then it's all figurative.
Then it's literal.

Private property's a puzzle too: wake to hermit thrush, cheerful eerie earful,
and if there's a fence between you and him, hard cheese, keep out, no chance
    to enhance
appreciative embodiment of dawn's airy airs, proximity limited, unless one
    breaks the law,
hops the fence, if it's a wood one, if it's barbed, don't opt for hopping, go for
    old clothes,
not too baggy, a pair of canvas work gloves, squeeze slowly through,
if you get snagged, don't panic and pull, that's how you tear things, including
    yourself,
if it's electric, watch the bare skin, that zap can zing you, and not in a good way
when power's turned up, this is not another anti-fence polemic, your neigh-
    bors have cattle,
Herefords up the road, Angus across it, you want them segregated, not on
    your doorstep
one Tuesday morning, almost two dozen cropping up cud, this is not attacking
holy cows of capitalism, lots of smart people have smart things to say
on salutary side-effects of the right to exclude from your personal turf, it's
    really just a question
of whether the trees would be better off if someone would talk to them, pat
    the bark of each
during drought especially, come on, old girl, you can do it, a few more weeks
of thirsting won't kill you, not after two centuries already weathered, if stud-
    ies show

how houseplants thrive on people's singing, then something analogous must
   go for trees,
we've got to get out there, croon to the saplings, counteract pollutants, acid
   rain irritants,
the stress of high winds, no payment is sought for services rendered, happy
   to do it,
it comes with the syndrome, but what say we skip prosecution for trespassing
and forgo petitions that ask for forgiveness, trees need love too, so does the
   creek
rain reinvigorates, you think I'm projecting and anthropocentric, another
   textbook basket case
of the poor pathetic fallacy's poor pathetic phallus, but wait, think it out,
   everything that is
has somehow adapted or it wouldn't be here, singing or howling or leafing or
   blooming,
and if it's adapted within my vicinity, then it's adapted to yours truly too, not
   that it's tame,
defanged, or domesticated, but its fields of force, electromagnetic, so that
   includes rocks,
cliffs, ledges, outcrops, its fields of force must overlap mine as I walk by, so
   as I walk by
there's mutual influence, it works on me at some micro-level, oxygen ex-
   haled,
radiation intercepted, the amount of iron ore embedded within it, and I
   work on it,
vibrating ground we have in common, the warmth of my panting having
   climbed up to it,
evaporating sweat moistening its air, the thousand bacteria fingertips leave,
sound waves' soft buffets if I address it or the bird in its branches or spring
   sky beyond,
some of this influence will surely be neutral and some may be harmful I'm
   sorry to say,
though not like a chainsaw or road bulldozed through, but some of the influ-
   ence
must benefit something and not only me, though what's beneficial for a
   rock's hard to say,
harder than what it could be for a tree, though even a rock is part of arrange-
   ment

constantly changing (almost crushed a stink bug within easy reach, then
    decided not to)
and giving off something amidst all the change, some emanation instru-
    ments can register,
Hans Geiger's counter is only one instance, but what if one made of oneself
such an instrument, to register rocks, their hummings and buzzings, this
    would be okay
with science, no need for atavism back to primitive animism, snicker,
    snicker, sniff, sniff,
imagine those primitives ever believing rocks have souls worthy of worship,
    guffaw, guffaw,
we're so far beyond that, where's my phone, I can't get reception, but maybe
    animism
was merely first description, an early attempt by sensitive instruments to say
    what they felt
in the presence of emanations, to say they felt fully in the presence of ema-
    nations,
and if, by a transitive law, they reasoned that rocks' sensible emanations
resemble those of living creatures, vibes will be vibes, rocks must be living
    too,
who the heck can blame them, our imaginations do much weirder things,
    you should meet
the people I work for, more about them below, but for now to return to
    private property,
it looks a little odd swamped with emanations, unfenced, unfencible, but
    odd isn't bad,
and as for preservation, what can it mean when everything's changing, and
    as for any nature
with no trace of man, what can that mean, since man's been emanating,
    woman maybe more so,
since the beginning of all men and women, their traces fainter in some
    places, sure,
but fainter's still there and never the same as absolute absence. Ask a prin-
    cess re a pea.

Why does the stink bug
push his luck and reappear,
the crushed smell not bad?

Sky's out, sun's blue, birds still sing, what's wrong with you?
How does anyone ever get on to the ultimate questions, God, love, death, art,
when that starter question's such a stumper, How are you, yo what's happening,
que pasa, comment ça va, sure, it's a greeting, a friendly formality, the pass-
    erby password,
sign, countersign, but once in a while somebody asks who seems to be seri-
    ous
and won't be brushed off by a breezy bien, then what, what then, now you're
    stuck
with having to figure it out for yourself, how am I doing, and where do you
    start
once you've checked in with a few simple basics, e.g., I'm not under gunfire,
scheduled for torture, or starving in famine, maybe it's best to move on
    quickly
to results of the lab work, your blood sugar, liver, and kidney functions
were once again excellent, your cholesterol was 168 and your LDL choles-
    terol 75,
both very good numbers, your iron level and blood count were normal,
as was your thyroid function, your PSA test for prostate cancer, ooh here we
    go,
was completely normal as well, phew, in summary, I think you are doing well
and once again suggest no changes at this time, there you go, that answer the
    question?
maybe you could print it on little beige cards, pin one to your hat
and say vide supra or pin one to your fly and say vide infra, maybe the in-
    quirer
will then walk away, chuckling heartily and saying what a wit a card a clown
or maybe what an asshole, heavily armored, completely defended in full-
    blown denial,
and she could be right, but what do you do if the answer's not simple or easy
    to abbreviate,
thank you for asking, I'm really not sure, if I didn't know better I'd have to
    admit
my false self is dying, there, you said it, was it so hard, my false self is dying
a slow smelly death, not a strong good one, as Stoics would have it, nor is it
    dignified
by learned last words or quotable wisdom others could live by, what's even
    worse

I've signed the directive, cut off all life-support, the drives for survival,
affection, esteem, the big respirators, reward, recognition, nothing is left
but the morphine drip to fuzz out discomfort, now that the group or role I
    identify
my drooling self with no longer answers, but still that tough sucker hangs in
    there kicking
and won't let it go, won't bow out gracefully, bargaining continues, O please
    greatest Pharaoh,
let me keep making bricks for your tomb, I don't need the straw, or yes I still
    do
but don't let it fret your fabulous Pharaohness, I'll find my own straw and
    still make the bricks
same as I used to and welcome the lashings should I fall short, just please let
    me keep
a few crumbs of pride, the spiritual kind if you don't mind, and maybe some
    reflections
back now and then, my name on papyrus, a few fawning fans, long live the
    false self,
it's got me this far, thank you for asking, how's Lent for you?

I: Why the white net?
She: I study colonies
of bees collapsing.

Holy Week at last and you'd never know it, jockeying for place, right-only
    lane,
Monday morning rush hour, *Stoßzeit* in German, a much better name, push-
    time
shove-time thrust-time punch-time shock-time, not by bread alone but by
    every word
in the dictionary, would that work, so many dictionaries, think of all the
    languages,
sixty-eight hundred, not all with lexicons but surely enough to engineer
    rapture,
ask for a sign and there's the green arrow, your turn to turn, but you could
    still die
because off to starboard, right-angled to you, somebody else with a green
    arrow too

pulls a quick U-ee, the yield-to-us sign having been missed or simply dis-
   missed,
not all his fault, it's poor traffic-planning, but don't bother writing a letter of
   complaint,
wait for the survey, your time is valuable, truly we know it, it takes a few
   minutes,
please check the box under your answer: while driving to work is a good
   time to pray,
strongly agree, somewhat agree, you gotta be kidding me, there's no box for
   that one,
how satisfied are you with your personal capacity for deep satisfaction,
   somewhat dissatisfied,
very dissatisfied, does it make a difference the sky is clear the sun is shining,
please feel free to add any comments, if you have questions, write this ad-
   dress,
she had a question, young woman yesterday, went something like this, why
   should we talk
so much about the Bible, nobody knows it, how does it help us understand
   better
Emerson Whitman Dickinson Thoreau, dactyl-then-trochee, dactyl-then-
   trochee
(that's how he said it). Nobody knows it? Can that be true, think of all the
   Bible camps,
Bible schools, college courses, study groups, seminars in seminaries, think of
   all
(changing lanes here) the growth in Africa, indigenous evangelism now sow-
   ing more
than missionaries ever did, what's that about, what it's about is it's never easy,
it's never been easy, to live with believing in things you can't see, if it were
   easy,
there wouldn't be scriptures, we'd all just believe, people'd quit talking
about their believing, same as your heartbeat, you don't discuss it, you don't
   even notice it
until something's wrong with it, then you start talking and talking right
   quick,
but once upon a la-la time, in la-la land so far away, everybody believed and
   nobody didn't,
hooey, humbug, baloney, my eye, the history of apostasy must be as old

as the second commandment, make God invisible and also abstract, what do
    you expect
when there's so much to see and stare at instead, people's heads turn, focus
    takes work,
attention's a discipline, what do you expect when attention disorder's trium-
    phantly pandemic
(now turning left), millions of images clicked on to choose from, what do
    you expect
believing to do but move to a continent with much less to choose from, less
    to distract
attention from basics, less to inflate the self to an idol (tough intersection
    here),
so belief has moved on, leaving the west awash in its images, in money and
    comfort,
though some still hang on and look pretty silly, but did they have road rage
in Nazareth of Galilee, would he have felt it, afoot or a-donkey,
you think it unlikely, prince of peace, turning his cheek, but what about
    Monday,
the last one he lived, when cleansing the temple, scourging the moneychangers,
he gave El Greco something to think about, five times he painted it, couldn't
    stay away
from the one use we see of physical force. (My favorite parking place.)

Flowering dogwood,
for a tree that God stunted
you look pretty good.

Last call. Last chance. Last will and testament. Last of the big spenders.
    Famous last words.
How about their weather, 79 degrees, sunny and warm, 51 percent humidity,
    wind from the west
10 miles per hour, no chance of rain today tonight tomorrow day after. Last
    of the Mohicans.
Last Year at Marienbad. Last Train to Clarksville. Last one in's a rotten egg.
    People talk
of climate change in Palestine, how it used to be greener, when a tree falls
in deforestation with no one there to hear it, does it still yell last gasp, last
    rites,

it can't last much longer, George Perkins Marsh, native Vermonter, American minister
to Turkey and Greece, warned the New World, 1864, annus horribilis, year of the
Wilderness, Spotsylvania, Cold Harbor, against the Old's track record, those parts that cut
down their moist forests and doing so changed their fair and fertile regions
into barren desert, Asia Minor, North Africa, there's rain in the Bible, no doubt about it,
aside from Noah's forty days, and people talk about it lots, but it's a dry haul
from rainy season at the end of Ezra to when it falls on Paul in Malta, three whole years
of preaching and healing and walking around and not once, not one single time
do we see rain fall on the unsheltered Teacher, it's no wonder, given their weather stats,
Ben Gurion Airport, maybe forty minutes from downtown Jerusalem, a cab'll run you
180 shekels, give or take, sunrise today 6:22, sunset this evening 7:02, seven hours difference,
so that's noonish our time, but don't say it that way, not in the Bible, say the sixth hour,
same as they do in rural Tanzania, so 7 p.m. would be, let's see, hour thirteen, never see that one
in the Good Book either, both Mark and Luke allude to sunset, but only once each,
and we never get to watch him watch it, never, nor do we see him out in the moonlight,
the moon, come on, the sine qua non of Passover, Nisan, the month of our redemption,
and yet he never mentions it, except as a sign and only three times, nor do our narrators,
but full moon, come on, the 14th of Nisan, that means full moon in Gethsemane also,
that means he's awake in the blaze of its rays, that means his friends, the closest he had,
slept through its light, no roof for excuse, what are we to do with such blasting silence,

how do we read in the maze of that muteness, Wycliffe, Tyndale, Coverdale, others,

oh yes the King Jamesers, gave us the chance to read for ourselves, but how do we go

about the blank parts, in which we're illiterate, whatever's hushed up still Greek to us,

read all the words however you have to, literal, figurative, or move to a view

beyond that distinction, but till we hear silence as full-blooded speech we think

something's missing, it's all a big hoax, turn up the sound, pop in your ear-buds,

saturate the supermarket with sonic pollution, subjugate shoppers to mind-less acoustics,

in the country of cacophony silence is resistance, closing in on noon here,

sunset in Jerusalem, last straw, last ditch, last minute, last supper.

Episcopalians
on their ways to foot-washings
check their pedicures.

How beautiful are the feet of them that preach the gospel of peace. Say what you want,

the King James team knew how to bring it, ti-tum-ti-ti-tum-ti-tum-ti-tum-ti-tum-ti-tum-ti-ti-tum,

a shape that hooked George Handel's ear, air for soprano before any pho-nemes

started to rollick, watch me alliterate, check out this consonance, final chias-mus of s and p

giving hard g, lone glottal stop, a stable balanced home, and don't forget that ménage à trois

of assonating e's, Easter day three, forty-seven more, and maybe there's good reason

to roll out the Mother's Day cards, move on, after all Paul revises Isaiah, mountains dropped out,

says nothing of peace in his Greek to the Romans, and never outrightly cor-rects misimpressions

that time in the tomb lasted three days, it didn't, stone into place by sun-down Friday

and then rolled away by sunup Sunday, thirty-six hours, absolute max, maybe
    even fewer,

enter the Enlightenment, then Feuerbach, Strauss, don't give to God what's
    rightly ours,

we want it back, no more divinity outsourced offshore, worship stays here,
    demystify deity

down to the boundaries of our local minds, anthropogenic, amen, alleluia,
    have another drink,

have a new prescription filled, still afflicted with nagging traces of vestigial
    devotion?

no problema, cue the Alzheimer's, shipshape that atheism, or is it just indif-
    ference,

if God's in the mind, then bring down the mind and watch God go with it,
    what was said

about attention, pandemic disorder, needs some revision, you should have
    seen

the old folks last night, listening, listening, one lady there a hundred and
    one, is she still sharp?

not all the time and she forgets things, repeats herself too, but you should
    have seen her,

the other ones with her, no phones or screens, nowhere to get to, nothing
    left to do,

just pure attention, fixed, unshakable, too bad the poems weren't any better,

same goes for inmates, try it out, you'll see, they won't get distracted, you are
    their distraction,

or not really you but what you stand in for, scuffed shoes and all, then there's
    the ashram,

5:30 wake-up, Satsang at 6, Pranayama, Selfless Service, Evening Satsang,

live like that for two or three years, suddenly your résumé looks pretty puny,

suddenly your demystifying's doubtlessly demystified, then our Lord stopped

and would not teach me any more until he had given me the grace and the
    will

to pay attention, sing it, Sister Julian, underline it too, but what about the
    precious set

of things we catch despite inattention, maybe because of it, five days ago,
    driving at sunset,

full moon rising, Pink Moon, Egg Moon, Sprouting Grass Moon, spacing out,
    there it was.

One score and ten years,
never seen one here before.
Should I report it?

Commas splicing, participles dangling, and oh those run-ons run-ons run-ons,
don't change the subject, there it was, tell us what, the thing about a revela-
    tion,
it often wrecks your skepticism, maybe even totals it, insurance adjuster
    comes out to look,
snaps a few pictures, hands you a check, there you go, that should cover it,
the Blue Book value of most incredulity, much cheaper for him than all the
    repairs
to get your indifference back on the road, scoffing intact, remaining dents
    hammered
out of secularity, hold on there, pal, wait just a second, things can reveal to
    the secular too,
however nullifidian, even the irreverent can have their wits tickled once in a
    while
by flashes of coincidence, uncanny surprises, deeper disclosures, no doubt
    about it,
and that's a big bonus, so much cardamon, clove, cayenne to fire up the
    familiar,
but once it's been digested, whatever's left passed through, it's back to the
    normal,
theophany's a different matter, a different brand of revelation, very few seek
    it
or seem all that happy when it comes upon them, Moses, for instance, mind-
    ing his business
along with Jethro's sheep, hid his face and tried to shirk, Jonah made a break
    for Tarshish,
even Paul, paradigm of quick conversion, afterwards wandered Arabian
    desert
and put off Jerusalem for three blank years, nothing recorded, getting a grip
    on what to do now,
women fare better it seems, if, especially, they're also named Mary, and like
    a pro burglar
what's undefined can always break in, with or without a capital letter, despite
    our locks,

with or without a church or a creed, despite our alarms, it's not a matter of
    whether or not
the undefined's out there, wherever that is, it's really a matter of if one's receptive,
not saying eager, but simply receptive, which if one's not, then they pass by,
lesser flickers of the undefined, without any notice, without any fuss, please
    pass the ketchup
and take out the trash, to each his own way toward an obituary, to each her
    own share
of purring and screaming, it can be like that, for most maybe is, but if one's
    receptive
things can crop up, there isn't much time, this will soon end,

it's so onerous,
this ongoing voice-over
one-upping itself,

but I've enjoyed it, not always, that's true, but I've learned quite a lot, about
    many things,
and feel somewhat better than when it all started, August last year, and last
    time we spoke,
he sounded okay, funny and upbeat, but one counts on nothing, don't count
    no higher,
and vis-à-vis nothing, there's a new oscillation (Bacchic etymology for that
    one, you'll see),
La Nada it's called, really the absence of other oscillations, El Niño, La Niña,
    the potent Pacific
contributing zip to constraining the jet stream, so the jet stream can thrash
    about as it pleases,
hence wild weather, heat waves and cold snaps and oh those tornadoes,
    childhood phobia
since Dorothy in Kansas, scary stuff a nightmare's made of, Scrooge's ghost of
    the future too,
but if future includes a death in a blizzard or in a freak hailstorm, that would
    be acceptable,
better than disease or car crash by far, weather at last ascending the throne,
    no longer demeaned
as subject for small talk, but now all one needs of dogmas and creeds,
    theophany abounding,

just ask a lawyer (though not if he's billing), the wilder the weather, the more
    Acts of God

for tort law and contracts, legal terminology revealing our theology, the more
    Acts of God,

the fuller the temples, churches, mosques, you want a big crowd, forget the
    evangelizing,

get yourself a hurricane, Category 5 will fill the pews fast, we're really so
    simple

when shove comes to scourging, earthquakes and floodings foster repen-
    tance, move over, Lent,

but what's repentance, which has a bad name and means more than guilt, so
    sorry, so sorry,

it means change of mind, that Greek metanoia, or change of heart, inten-
    tion, purpose,

or think of it as meta-heart, heart beyond the one thumping now, a little too
    fast during disaster,

and between disasters, apparently coming at shortening intervals, the
    weather beats anything

offered on a screen, just take the wind, first off it's free, available to all who
    aren't in a hospital

or correctional facility, then think what it offers acousticophiliacs, in breezes
    or gales

leaves talking dirty, or how odors differ, depending on direction, musky or
    scorched,

lemon or leather, there it is now, north window open, tickling the neck,
    tonguing an ear,

this morning woke up to a white-throated sparrow, It's All Marvelous Mar-
    velous Marvelous,

kept up the singing at least half an hour, fine way to start a forgettable day,
  . wind's picking up

the last thirty seconds, sky's darker too, this isn't digression, I saw what I saw.

The stink bug who passed
last night in a water-glass
got swallowed first thing.

Why should it surprise, any kind of mind-change, or any change at all
reversing our direction, the needles on our compasses pointing south instead,

not the simple fickleness of changing minds about martinis, sorry for the
hassle,
make mine with onions instead of with olives, but changes on the order of
what I once thought
wrong I now am thinking right, what I once thought bad now I think is good,
useless useful,
dead alive, it happens all the time, apparently, not just the Sundays after full
moons
after vernal equinoxes, compass needles swinging south not, in fact, a metaphor
or mere analogy but molten-cored Earth's pole reversal, markings on the
compass rose,
hundreds of thousands of years ago, off by half the circle, our planet, bipolar,
having flipped magnetic fields hundreds of times in three billion years, no
big deal
say fossil records or ocean-bottom lava flows, no fearful fodder
for doomsday connoisseurs, just constant inconstancy, think of all the orien-
tations
suddenly in need of full revision, the toilet flushed or bathtub unplugged
swirling in the opposite direction (no, doofus, your bathroom vortex has
nothing to do
with magnetic poles or Earth's rotation, see Coriolis, which puts its spins on
weather systems,
one way north, the other south), magnets on fridges will suddenly jump, and
walks in the woods
will call for new compasses or call, at least, for new affection for getting lost,
not so hard to imagine these changes, pretty minor when you get down to it,
but what about the Aymarans up in the Andes, the ones with the language
that places the past
in front of its speakers, the future in back, not so simple as flipping your
needle
to make the adjustment to putting your troubles before you while looking
behind
to much better times, though many do in English, true, but not in a spirit of
hopeful expectance,
think of futurity over your shoulder, the past dead ahead, it makes lots of
sense,
things done we can see, things undone we can't, but now who are we,
forward-thinkers,

and what will happen to making our plans, to providence, prudence, the
     avant-garde
now bringing up the rear, where's Heaven now, better get in on the soon-to-
     boom market
among the ass-backward off in their backwaters.

At dawn they cross paths,
doe in woods out the window,
two gobblers, fans spread.

It's not so bad, really, among the ass-backward, off in our backwaters,
we the ass-backward in various states, in order to form imperfect connec-
     tions
with the dominant ethos of constant connection, hereby acknowledge and
     even admire
(there's the wood-thrush, often audible drizzly mornings), even admire the
     line of thinking
dedicated to the proposition that constant connection makes all people equal
and all people free to connect as they please, especially valuable for people
     who live
where others interfere with some of their freedoms or people immobile,
     shut-in, sick
for whom a small screen means keys to a kingdom, huzzah, let's hear it
for constant connections that meliorate lives, so long as one's free, just as
     free, let's hear it,
not to connect with the dominant ethos for no other reason than that it's the
     dominant
and some prefer not to, as long as there's freedom, submit to domination
when twenty-two lady slippers at last count await, up on the ridge, for count-
     ing again
this late April morning before they disappear, the annual booty of small yel-
     low booties
gone for a year and maybe forever, if logging comes in in the intervening
     months
or one should succumb, during those months, to that other succumbing,
     definition two
(Carolina wren, close to the house, so clearly obstreperous), this isn't senti-
     mental

attachment to the past or over-idealizing some pastoral utopia, which never
    existed,
as defenders of the dominant quickly point out, in fact it's purely practical,
a limited number of minutes in hours, hours in days, days in lives, one has to
    choose
and choosing means letting some choices go, not with condemnation or
    dishonorable discharge
but simply because one doesn't have time or a suitable sensorium, the seat of
    sensation
already hot and risking overheating, for piling more connections on top of
    vigilance needed
to mark the first cicada, due back again, seventeen years since the last batch
    evaporated.

Let my people go,
or if they'd rather stay here,
let me go alone.

Sure, this is politics, what else could it be, and some will contend that citi-
    zens connected
are responsible citizens, doing the work of civic engagement, while those
    unconnected
because of cicada or wood-thrush or lady slipper have retreated reprehensibly
into privileged aristocracy, into ostrich detachment that made Hitler pos-
    sible, if ever in doubt
use Hitler in an argument, nobody else shakes logic up faster, though some
    come so close
it's hard to resist and say wait a minute, if it's so healthy, so conducive to
    freedom
for all to be connected, then why does connection produce uniformity,
    people connected
mostly look the same, tell someone from Mars, recently landed, oh no Mr.
    Martian,
you've got it all wrong, even though inhabitants of this warming planet ap-
    pear to be trained
to sit very still in front of small rectangles, leashed by the ears to something lit up,
each one is really a study in freedom, innovation, not just a node of tranquil-
    ized docility

connectors can manipulate, I see, I see, says the Martian enlightened, now I
understand,

Connection Macht Frei (a bilingual Martian), so let's drop the Hitler move,
it's just a cheap shot,

and consider instead the division of labor, how for every young woman who
keens I'd be lost

(this happened yesterday) without the latest phone, or for every hundred
thousand,

including guys too, there have to be a few for whom the technology of bird
song's sufficient,

a few who get assigned, unless they volunteer, to full-time engagement with
rain on a Thursday,

with night sky unclouded or silence in a crowd, this is not a referendum on
the value of tools

many use productively, bring on more tools, more arts, more skills, and don't
let us burden them

with having to save us, toys are tools too, it's okay to wield them for nothing
but pleasure

without always fretting how someone's getting rotten rich off someone else's
wielding

or dreading a day when someone decides the freedom to wield must be
curtailed,

it's not a referendum, it's a question of balance, in any healthy system there
has to be difference,

think of dogs breeding, you want healthy hips in litters they issue, keep them
away

from brothers and sisters, same humping same can lead to bad things, there's
more fun to milk

from this canine comparison, you can be the Saint Bernard, I'll play Chihua-
hua

(had to look it up, never typed it out before), but let us move on in the inter-
est of time,

despite time's disinterest in any of us, and turn to the words in the last dream
this morning,

chanted they were and went something like this, Delight, Delight, Wherever
it is low,

Go fill it from the sun, Or turn it down low, no, that's exactly how they went,
had to fight back

the urge to revise or try to evade identical rhyme, especially given the ser-
   mon on difference,
but that's how they went, scout's honor, heart crossed, really quite lovely, the
   tone of the chant,
it was worth working hard to hang on to the words, everything else flown
   from the mind.
Damn, I keep forgetting to tell you what I saw.

What a bonanza,
but would it have been better
if there'd been stanzas?

May Day, mayday, all hands on deck, mayhap, mishap, Mayflower Compact,
enough of this mayhem, I'm running for mayor, so glad to see you, I hope I
   can count
on your vote in November, don't be dismayed, there's still lots of mayonnaise
and plenty of maypoles, workers of the world unite, general strike, maybe
   just maybe
I shouldn't have drunk that forbidden cup, caffeine prohibited, I thought it
   would help
focus the finale, now I'm not sure, things kind of jumble, yeehah what a
   rush,
my youth is renewed, rejuvenation, that's tricky too, days by the dozen
   youth's not so great,
at least not for some, at least not for one, let's don't go there, let us go some-
   where,
Carolina wren, thunderstorm this morning, let us go somewhere, I'll take
   you there, hang on
hang on, country road curves, not much for shoulders, tough place to learn,
   I've got the wheel,
right about here, four weeks ago, as I was saying, we're back on the track, full
   moon a-rising
opposite sunset, not a bad day, though not quite a joyride, and then there it
   was
in a field taking off, driver's side window, but doing fifty-five, age and veloc-
   ity,
it's hard to be sure, looked like a vulture, they're common, it's true, and not
   very pretty

encountered close up, though sailing on updrafts they can be stirring, not
    very pretty

but this one was different, seeming white feathers against the green grasses,

not likely here, this isn't their habitat, no way, it can't be, around the next
    curve

made a U-turn, not very safe, but there comes a time one's ready to go, not
    seeking the end

but not scared of it either, the peace has been made, the seeds have been
    sown, let someone else

take over the show, made the U-turn and on the retrace got a full view, wings
    unmistakable,

flat spread beheld, the white hood in profile, crossing the road, and then it
    veered north,

ahead of the car and next for a furlong what's a furlong who cares it sailed
    straight away

leading the way, ahead of the bumper two or three car lengths, filling the
    windshield,

harder to see in some ways through tears, easier too when youth is renewed

when thy youth is renewed, it says, like an eagle's

ACKNOWLEDGMENTS

Thanks to William Thompson and Patricia Waters, who published Part 1 of this poem in the *Alabama Literary Review.*

Grateful appreciation to the Office of the Dean of the College of Arts and Sciences and the Vice President for Research and Graduate Studies, University of Virginia, for timely support.

After nearly two decades my editorial debt to John Easterly is deep.

To each of those who read this book at various stages, a beholden bow.

CPSIA information can be obtained at www.ICGtesting.com
Printed in the USA
BVOW04s0102291114

376945BV00002B/13/P